WHOLE SKY

WHOLE SKY

by
Pamela Kircher

FOUR WAY BOOKS
Marshfield

Copyright © 1996 Pamela Kircher

No part of this book may be used or reproduced in any manner without written permission except in the case of brief quotations embodied in critical articles and reviews. Please direct inquiries to:
Editorial Office
Four Way Books
PO Box 607
Marshfield, MA 02050

Library of Congress Number 95-061372

ISBN 1-884800-10-6

Cover painting, watercolor by Fulvio Testa, 1989
Text design by Acme Art, Inc.
Manufactured in the United States of America

This book is printed on acid-free paper.

Four Way Books is a division of Friends of Writers, Inc., a Vermont-based not-for-profit organization.

ACKNOWLEDGEMENTS

"Ars Poetica" and "Perceptible Breath" were originally published in braille on a sculpture called "Vanitas," by Todd Slaughter. The sculpture is permanently installed in the atrium at the Columbus Metropolitan Library, Columbus, Ohio.

Acclaim: "Perceptible Breath"; *The American Poetry Review:* "By the Lilies," "Desperate Angel" (revised), "Dream of the Rest of My Life," "Every Night," "Without End" (revised); *Calapooya Collage:* "One River"; *The Fourway Reader #1:* "Alba," "Ars Poetica," "In Which a Single Answer Is Given to Two Questions...," "In Which the Insomniac Finds Dreams," "Looking at the Sea," "Whole Sky"; *Garland Edition*, Heatherstone Press, 1981: "The Heartland" (revised); *The Georgia Review:* "Intimate Earth" (republished in *Keener Sounds, Selected Poems from The Georgia Review,* 1987); *The Ohio Review:* "Alba" (revised), *"Looking at the Sea,"* (republished in *Best American Poetry* 1993); *Sycamore Review:* "A Kind of Goodbye"; *Tar River Poetry:* "No Telling"

Some of these poems were written with the support of fellowships from the Ohio Arts Council and the MacDowell Colony.

Contents

Liar	1
Dream of the Rest of My Life	3
Without End	4
Pretending I Am My Lover, I Write Myself:	5
Multiple Souls	6
In Answer to My Friend Asking What I Think of My Death	10
Explaining My Sadness	12
Redbird Sings	13
Go to Dark	16
Ars Poetica	17
Night in a Room	18
Dreamer's Dark	20
Looking at the Sea	22
In Which the Insomniac Finds Dreams	24
Whole Sky	26
What You Remember of Love While Looking at Photographs	30
By the Lilies	31
Desperate Angel	32
What Some of Us Don't Know:	33
We Love the Moon So It Shines	35

Black Weed 36
Every Night 37
Perfect Stillness 38
A Kind of Goodbye 40
The Intimate Earth 42
No Telling 43
Perfect in Its Purpose 44
One River 45
Alba 47
Perceptible Breath 48
The Dark Ones Are Here to Help 49
The Skin's Resistance 51
The Heartland 53
Finding a Dream 55
Maybe Not What You Want or What You Lost 56
Two Women Talking 58
In Which a Single Answer Is Given to Two
    Questions: How Big Is a Heart and
    How Much Can It Hold? 59
Manatee 61

Liar

One white hand
held up before the light,
finger-bones and chips of nail
thin as fish-scales at the ends,
and flesh. Even with two
stray hands brought together
into a cup for water, into a boat
for air to sail away in,

I come up empty
at night, a child again
in bed, in summer,
the window open and heat
like a beast beside me. Fireflies
in a jar on the floor
won't light up, are almost dead
and will be dead by morning.
Such certainty

of wings and husks
inside the jar is why I know I'm only
one thing in this world, one
with a bad name at that,
what you say now, holding me,
now releasing me
to the night

where what little breeze there is
clings to the leaves of trees
leaving me untouched and waiting
for fireflies to light up inside my hands
because the liar I am
promised me some sign, some absolute
proof of love.

Dream of the Rest of My Life

Last night
I dreamed I had been alone
all of my life:
it was evening by railroad tracks,
a brick building, a window I looked in
at myself. The woman I saw there was not happy
but used to the empty white room

where nothing was ever given
or taken away. I could tell
this was a woman who never woke in the night,
went to the window and looked up the road
for the person who should have been home
hours before. Since I have chosen you

I stand at the window and watch a turn in the road
until it becomes a blur, a wish for headlights
pushing the night aside.
For the rest of my life
I will wake in the morning and wonder
as the sun lays a ribbon across the floor,

what can I use it for
quick before it goes
and why do I want it so much
when it means your shadow and mine
will be less like ourselves
as the days pass on, will be longer,

more like a cloth to step into
and draw about our shoulders, faces, heads,
when we each, alone, are tired.

Without End

Rain for weeks keeps us from speaking.
The tv screen flashes a map of disaster,
houses listing like ships, fences and fields broken down
into flotillas of sticks.
                      What is happening to us
is the question laid at my feet by the river
creeping across the road with its cargo of mud.
You're up to your knees in it,
salvaging scrap for possible use
when the water recedes and the mess
is something you can haul away,
dry out, shore up.
                My face reflects in water,
indecisive and blank. I recognize the hesitation
before complete destruction: eye of the storm,
and river's crest, a heart's troubled pump when it holds
more than its measure of grief. Five bluebirds
dead on the bank, black beaks,
rose breasts the color of eyelids on the inside,
pressed closed.
                A thousand mistakes
drift in a life and a life brought close
by desire, by chance without end.
When the river slips back in its bed
you kneel by the house, lift and stake
the gladiola, rinse their red lips

not looking at me
since turning your face away
is the only available grace.

Pretending I Am My Lover
I Write Myself:

I do not want you anymore.
The moon begins to frighten me
moving with such certainty each night
before it turns around, changes place
and face again.

Like you it is mostly hiding
and like you is mostly not
the sphere, the crooked smile and bright white
I follow sleeplessly across the sky

onto the brink of morning
and the falling of a thousand lights.
You make a beauty of confusion
with your lips, make desperateness
desire when you lie down.

When you're asleep, I realize
you're terrible; you find order
in the destruction that you make.
Is this why you refuse
to close the curtains by the bed?

You let the moonlight wander in
and touch the floor, your face and hands;
you let it change the room each night
and make you what it will.

Multiple Souls

1.

Suffocating August evening,
after dinner, just dark,
a girl lay in damp grass watching cigarettes
redden like small planets and go out.
Swifts circled above the house
and dropped one by one into the chimney.
The perfect beginning, night

with its multiple souls. The girl
looked up through miles of air, not breathing
as she counted stars and gathered them
into birds and fish, each a beast
she could lose her heart to
when they sparked
 but they went out
because the hostess turned on lights.
Grownups bobbed about on chairs and blinked,
having surfaced, I know now,
from some disquieting place.

2.

Lights open as I go checking things out,
bedroom to basement. Still,
when the refrigerator jumps on
I jump too, assume

that the gloved hand fondles the knob,
that someone is about to tap on the glass
when I walk through the hall to bed

not looking behind doors, into rooms,
at the window where a face floats
but is not my own.

I lie down, close my eyes, abandon
the vessel to the eddy of gray and black,
the interior whirlpool

until the screen door slams
open and I wake emptied
of breath, heart drowning all sound

and the man who has waited so long
moves to the bottom stair.
One hand holds the rope
and one hand rubs his crotch
like a lucky stone.

3.

I wake and there you are,
turned toward me beneath the covers,
outline of shoulder, hip, knees, feet,
perpetually vulnerable like me
to cold, knives, the delicate torture of husband-and-wife.
So much I could do to you
but your outstretched hand expects a kiss.
I push it away,
get up into mummified light.

Last night the whirlwind snow
haloed the mercury vapor lamps.
A man walked alone with his face turned up,
his open mouth catching miraculous snow.
I sat locked in; the cat tiptoed
in the room upstairs and yowled.

This morning snow
is like a handkerchief across a face.
It doesn't tremble, doesn't pulse or flutter
—who is dead in a house along this street?
I can't love you
when half the world is locked away,
when half the chambers of the heart are closed.

Through the window
a rabbit, flat and gray as a soul,
sits transfixed on the snow-covered lawn,
its two black eyes searching the two horizons.
Snow slips from the roof and the rabbit starts,
stands like a deathly stone,
not knowing what it expects to see
but expecting, already terrified.

4.

Street lights go on
and children playing hide and seek
hear a boy leave home base calling
all-come-free
as he walks up the block, arms waving,
but not really looking

for the places they hide:
down cellar stairs, beneath porches,
up in the branches of a tree where a girl holds fast
until night comes down and buoys her up. Darkness

begins its possibilities. Houses and trees edge away
and her mother gives up calling her name.
All around fireflies waver in air
and she wants to stay forever.
This is the way the world can be saved;

she is sure of it. Forgetting hands, mouth,
bone, plunging into dark-pounding,
into the double-barreled heart.

In Answer to My Friend Asking What I Think of My Death

After a hard freeze, a few mornings
of frail snow writhing under the whoosh of cars,
the sun

bores through gray, bleaches it blue,
making these
the warmest November hours.

Rime burns off. Wet leaves smoke,
lighten, lift with a misdirected southern wind,
coming for nothing.

For that reason I stop the car, step out
and over to the fence. Across the pasture

Holsteins, nose to tail, nose to tail,
wash to the barn. In a silence
a low moan from the cows touches me

before traffic noise beats again
over median strip and berm.

Another ending is here.
The past has and will disappear
like irises, not even a limp,
drained leaf remains.

The future is nothing but dirt
stove in by a cow's hoof,
overflowing with colorless air.

The future is no good

until green, weedy things strike up.
I measure myself with these.
I am one

in the round of silence,
    cacophonous color,
        silence
            shoving the starling's dry beak
            asunder.

Explaining My Sadness

More than anything that day we wanted
to be lovers. All along my spine, thighs
I felt whispers — yes

was the word, insistent hiss like hothouse steam,
stupefying like the cardinal's battering of glass resounding
with the crack of yes.

Possibility existed then in kisses.
Pigeons wheeled and flashed in accidental sun;
their shadows shattered on our heads and faces,
blew across the lawn. I wanted to believe and did
as we walked around a concrete pond.

(Oh, erratic
circle circumscribed by moths around a flame
—only half-crazed, only half-paralyzed),

do you sing, you asked; then on another pass
asked again, can you sing? (The answer is,
only when I'm alone). To you I said,
I can't,
and when you asked again
I said, I can't.

Then a wind fumbled for the trees;
the pond opened its unreflective eye.
I saw cans, plastic, a torn shoe

and the two shadows that we are
tried to touch but fell right through
to the wider arms of what is
beyond us all times.

Redbird Sings

1.

Five fingers,
short, knuckle-swollen and bent,
my grandmother's hand in my hand
as I sit looking past her at the window,
the square, gray sky that doesn't seem to move
but I know it's rushing past: the sky,
it's something, it's nothing.

With her fingertips she rubs the bones above her breasts,
she rubs her abdomen, her throat, her mouth;
she stares at the corner of the room
while her hands figure it out. She says,
"this is it," lifts her right hand,
taps her forehead and nods
as if an idea were present in the room, as if
her other hand could fish it out of air.

For five weeks
she has been trying to die
and every moment, breath
and not breath,
could be it. She knows
so when I cannot say goodbye
she clasps both hands around my neck,
says my name in a way I've never heard.

Her eyes and mine
seeing walls, window, sky,
a face now
but never again.

2.

Outside a window of her house,
chickadee and cardinal fight for seed,
a downy woodpecker lurches up
and down a branch of amputated lilac.
Six miles away she is dying,
propped in her hospital bed,
staring with stroke-struck eyes.
White. Red. Black.
I rattle the glass with my fist
and chickadee, cardinal startle away.
It is time they learn the difference.
When she is dead they will hop on icy sills;
they will be confused by the unmoved snow,
absence of suet, a stillness
behind the glass. From this window
a view of the place where birds
are out of sight, where
husband, mother, sister, father, brother
and I
will eventually fall, a well
of inescapable sky.

3.

Then she is dead. My father
sleeps on the couch. My mother,
exhausted, dry-eyed, has gone to bed.
No one would disturb this rest
of the living among the dead
but you and me
together in my childhood bed
are seized by the connections
of our bodies hip to hip,
lips and tongues, we screw
as if this were our own sanctuary

between the brittle sheets.
The impatient, slipshod bed
jerks and creaks, who cares
what anyone thinks of such a panic;
it is love.

4.

The irises came up three inches,
betrayed by a temporary warmth that left them
stranded, brown in a powdering of snow.
If they were human
it would demonstrate disaster
befalls the ones who act on first emotion,
it would prove my body leads me on
to my conclusion. Husband, do not touch me,
I want to stay intact inside my skin.
The redbird sings and sings but I'm not taken in.
Spring is a ruined season.
It will come, bedraggled, torn,
tossing its pale colors like confetti on the lawn,
begging to be caught and held.
No hope of it, no hands are adequate.
Nothing will match the imagined glory
of stripped and splintered irises.
The heart is implacable when it's robbed.

Go to Dark

woe to him who lives always
in the light if he does not go
to dark dark will come to him
yes

it is spring
grass turns all its being to green
and magnolia steps away from itself
to live in air
but not forever
the fragrant body dissipates
petals edge to brown and brittleness

the goddess turns another time
and never shows her face full

the choice is not between
this and that one thing or another
but how

to tell the viscera's story
twisting between light and dark
start and end

Ars Poetica

If you were born with your right hand trapped
in your left hand's clasp,

you have already fallen out of heaven
and must live. You will suffer questions;

every answer will be changed
by the breath that buoys it beyond recall,

and the truths you are given easily,
again and again,

are those you wish undone

as when a woman slips the white string from her wrist

and the blue balloon ascends
as silently as a solitary child

retreating up the stairs,
bearing just such a heart to bed,

to muffle it under covers, to be hidden
in the labyrinth of dream.

Night in a Room

1.

Outside the lighted room, a big raccoon wades on her toes
through the gray, her shoulders shrugged against opinion
of her face, her build, the waste
of her small, padded, pliable paws
at work in the trash
probing and caressing, releasing from bags and bundles
a tomato split and speckled with mold,
pork trimmings white as lace, pudgy as grubs:
she feeds.

She pats the bottom of the can in a small applause,
then stands, eyes just above the rim,
ears tuned to a back door. She waits,
pulls the gray sack her soul lives in to the edge
then topples the can with smack and clatter,

springing the porched dog from his coil of sleep to a spasm
of bark bark bark bark bar
as his master tourniquets his collar,
dribbles his front feet on the floor, drops and hits him
once because doesn't the dog know it's a coon?
Again, because how can he be so dumb?

2.

At night in a room lit by a small lamp,
the far white wall placid
as a low, full note just struck,
illuminating what was only air

the exact moment the eye unshutters
and finds the short-legged, slat-back chair
there against the wall.

I gaze at what it is:
patient frame, a thing, and possibility.
The way, I hope, my bones will be a thousand years on
when the exhumer speaks into the nothing that is left

of my ear questions,
like wind through eroded stone, asking

who ever used me and why? Where did I travel;
what dragged me back; who touched me and how did I
    hold anyone
wanting me knowing nobody needed me and I
was only myself?

Let him move through his speaking,
numbering my bones and bundling them,
urged by a chipmunk's wild, live eye to hold
and turn me once around the grave like an awkward
    partner
as I around my bed waltz coupled
with the stiff, uncompromising chair.

Dreamer's Dark

Daytime sleep makes clear the dark
where the woman dreams is different
from absence of light, separate

as the first world is from her room
where a fly measures her pillow in all directions
and prays beside the sleeper's vacant face.

She is gone, born briefly back through dream
to early evening long ago covered over
with doves' wings beating air till it cries

like the silent child never does,
sitting still at the table
with a white plate, a heap of peas,
and a carved chair's glare fierce
as a darning needle through silk.

The window reflects black
living room and beyond, a lighted porch.
Clumsy June bugs click against the ceiling fixture
and her mother concentrates on killing them.
The slap, silence, slap

of the newspaper sounds like the slowest step of a giant
finding the last, inhabited cave.

No one remembers this evening

the girl was told sit until you finish.
So she sits before the black hole of the window,
looks at the curtains, learns by heart the pattern

ravelling as sadness. She sings
as she scoops each cold pea with her spoon:

the silver fish is totally forgotten;
the silver fish is free; its eye is green
and wrinkled like an ocean wave
so everyone it sees is swept away.

Looking at the Sea

> *Stiff tone of death*
> *in every wave*
> *what more can wave have*
> *save perhaps a little love*
> Marsden Hartley

Not in anger does the sea
fold to the source of its gray waves
the tired boy; not in hatred
does it choke him.

Before and afterwards a weight
breaks each wave, but not remorse

nor does forgiveness move the tides
to coax the shriveled kelp and barnacles,
the stinking whelks to trust
the sea's embrace again.
We who travel with our feelings
can't believe the sea responds mechanically
to the earth's rotation or the moon
giving up another sliver every night.

White edging on the waves leads the eye
from horizon into shore, from rocks
to a plume of spray dissolving into blue
oblivion,

abandonment,
convincing evidence
that prior to this breath
we were protected;

just yesterday
seagulls sang like doves.

In Which the Insomniac Finds Dreams

As soon as I know the night means to be
a long walk in a narrow hall
and playing the refrigerator light
(on again off again on),

I'm in the car and driving fast
till in no time it's me and my mind

in the countryside on a long road
between corn fields and fences,
where towns are few and suddenly

there's a white-wood, window-boarded store,
three houses then tombstones
and the dead rising up in the twisting wind of me

passing through, me on the verge of the future
that flies up like a dove from the center line
and is instantly behind me again and again

until darkness

slips from the swift tilt of a swallow's wing,
until somewhere the wide eye closes
but never mine:

I feel dreams kicking like horses
in narrow stalls of sleep, keen
for me to slip the bolt, swing the door,

whistle them down the road.
They darken the night with dust,
break up the cup of silence with a bold tattoo;

they don't linger in fields of sleep
but gallop till they reach the eastern hill
where morning first loses its footing and falls
into this day

making horses gleam and holding them
like water on an autumn web.

I see how each dream begins and ends
as the red mare steps into the shadow
and back out without a thought of me.

I see between us

the field knotted with wild rose,
the tangle tightening
its grip on itself.

Whole Sky

I.

The wood is green layers of light and sheer leaf,
new leaf, another smooth leaf
and all the dark tattered ones
together

in untiring ascension in all directions,
becoming a stillness as big as the blue
the robin's song falls through

beginning and ending each day
like water in a slow and fretful drain.

What the sycamore crashes through
jerking its short roots out,
spurting up dirt, twisting and breaking its spiral of
    branches,
walloping the ground.

Beneath the weight of limp and drying leaves,
violets fade to white and wither,
changing as the present ruptures into being

steadily as a snake's newest scales
ready beneath the worn ones
until a crack, a snag, the startling

split and slip of bright, consoling beauty
spilling out red and yellow or green and buff,
mottled olive, amber spatters, oiled indigo

like the strip of sky towing the thunder and then
all black. I recognize
my life sliding forward past sticks and through
the crumpled shoots.

II.

The history of a rock is its weight,
its brittle edges incising the mothering air
and another side deep in blind
blunt nuzzling into dirt.
From this

think then of mountains as countries,
one river cliff a city,
the roadside rock-slide a family
and one loose stone shuttled along by this car and that
a person
a woman
a history
of hitting men.

I hit him and wouldn't stop when a friend said please.
Didn't stop for a black eye, goodbye, you bitch, a bruise
that spread like a lake into four fingers. We were alone
with the noise of breathing, body against body against walls
and the unsupporting air. Hear the word no stretch on
and on with nothing in itself
to stop it.

I made him go further than he ever wanted to with me

drag me by my ankles down metal stairs

slam me and my head for company
against the hallway wall
collapsing in muffling black
amazing with its little flotilla of white
flashes in front of me fading away

fantastic and funny

he half-collapses my windpipe and through the space
between his forearm and my neck-bone
my voice trickles out thin and bright as a wire

listen to this, oh, listen to this. We might be friends still,
we might be.

Shhh, they are sleeping, each on an edge
of the bed. She will wake and wait. He will wake
and take her one more time. That is all
to come. The speechless sheets huddle on the floor
having foretold it all in tangles and stains.

III.

I've been listening lately to the green
that comes out and dances the tips of trees,
the green being that thrusts up from the ground
translucent with yearning.

One rock making a whole stream change.
The pattern the bee waggles through telling a story
other bees must listen to. A meaning

when from far away the hummingbirds return in June
attacking with jab and feint and swoop, retiring to a wire
to lash with long and liquid tongues the unresponsive air.

I understand.
A hummingbird is never beautiful but agate-green and dull
until by accident it tilts and spills into the sun a rash of red,
a searing emerald
abrupt, astonishing

as memory of a green alley between backyards
where on weekdays the littlest kids
pried from the grass
bottle caps and pennies,
and left a certain child by a certain tree
tufted with thorns
whenever they could.
The space left around you after that

eats sound, so the memory is mute
except for green running on
in front and always right behind

as though the alley never ends.
The sun stays over it
like the flat of a hand on flesh,
but I don't remember me ever reaching
some place meant for turning
and coming home,
so envious already

of the rutted path with its puddles holding
the whole sky,
rocks white with the sun's erasure.

What You Remember of Love While Looking at Photographs

That the road escapes the mountains
into bleached land and long-horned cattle
grazing in grass. Air

empty as the soul is, and hot,
tasting of salt with a deep
blue eye over all that water. Veracruz

where bottles shine like knives on the beach,
crosses in a hollow church, fish
moving far down, beyond you.
That blind spot
where the sun comes up through water

and faith departs when the dark hands
leave your eyes, your body alone.

Then you see egrets in the long grass
shaking white plumes.

By the Lilies

Hot, the smell of tar paper, buzz of wasps,
all of us dragging the old buggy
through shed doors and bumping
across the grass to the stand of lilacs.
There were clothes for each of us,
long black skirts and for my brother,
brown trousers full of holes. I can remember
nothing of our play, only the smell
of hot, musty clothes, the baby buggy's
cracked leather hood, cracked tires.
Not one of us could fit inside it,
so it was useless and stood by me
by the lilies, scorched by summer, everyone run away
    leaving
the sound of crying and all the shades
in the house pulled down.

Desperate Angel

At night they must be walking
on the knives and spoons,
pissing and sniffing the spatula's thin edge
not knowing I sleep in another room,
having undressed once more, having lain down again
with the thought tomorrow. Between that
and the day's false start of simple light
is nothing but the furnace's senseless chunk
and hum. Open the drawer. Again
the trap is flung on its back,
the mouse wedged in beneath the wire
like a desperate angel squeezing into heaven.
The tail lays straight;
a last oval shit clings
to the white fur that ripples
beneath a breath.
Turn the head just right
and its eyes glint
as if some thought were caught
beneath its skull, familiar,
having nagged for days and days
and only given time
might make all the difference.

What Some of Us Don't Know:

I was five years old and hit my dog over the head with a
 board.

A good board for smothering weeds
and bedding slugs behind the garage.

Tomatoes hung at my head back there,
plummeted when I brushed them,
split to juice and pulp and sticky seed.

My sister remembers I hit him,
but not why;
I can't remember
but feel
cold inside my upper arms where someone
takes hold and shakes you,
and in my hipbones even though it happened
in summer. The school was empty then,
or almost so, or should have been.
Something bad

has to happen
for a child to slam a board
against her cocker spaniel's coppery head.

My sister remembers
the board's blunt, truncated arc
and the narrow-bladed yelp.
I can only imagine

before the board I touched
a tomato leaf and hated the smell, its unbright side
clasping the fruit. Beneath it
a hidden, thin shadow zippering the stalk
from root to tip.
I hated it.

The yelp sliced deep.
The dog went mean.
Sent to the pound he must have choked in a pen of gas
within a week.

Under the forsythia's fortress of branches
the dog chain nestled link by link by link
into the dirt,
covered deeper,
keeping me.

We Love the Moon So It Shines

There are things seen only
when the lights are off.
Like night shifting its ashes
through the house almost soundlessly
except for a sudden crack then later
a soft thud for all the world
like a shovel breaking a root and a clump of dirt
dropped in a hole. Being buried alive.
How simple. She touches the floor
with one foot, the edge of the bed
with one hand. There she is
in the mirror, hardly a woman at all:
crooked at the waist, one arm long,
one bent. She picks up her dress
from the floor and lays it over the man
in the bed. Let him wake
in the hours that come and find
what his lies have done. The body
of the blue dress as empty
as the lover she has become.
All the rest of her ugly and dumb
as the moon's far face waiting night
after night to turn to the earth
and shine.

Black Weed

Starlings peck wrinkled hawthorne fruit,
preen stiff wings and leave
the tree trembling along one or two branches
before it becomes still again,
fixed in its spot, branches rigid
in January air. Little
by little we're shown how one
touch sweeps away another, how
lips after kissing close
only on themselves again, and sleep.
Sucking a black weed from the bottom, the duck
paddles off. Scattering drops from the plant
disappear as the lake washes smooth
when the duck is gone, since nothing
was given and what was taken
would have died of itself in time.

Every Night

Washing her few spoons
over and over,
she lives her life.
Out back a railroad track
grows weeds with sticky leaves
and at the edge of the yard
stand heavy clubs of ironweed.
Every night the train
whistles through and in the silence
left behind with her
she feels how cleanly it pulled
itself free of here,
that somewhere else it rests
glistening and taut,
stripped like rabbits
on pink, damp newspapers
in her mother's kitchen.
She always thought
they looked smooth enough
to rub her cheek on,
and she would hold the bare bodies
in her hands and they were still,
free at last of their ticks and fleas,
the bramble-flight of nerves and startled breath
that even now catches her
with the spoons clattering in the sink,
the single bulb spluttering, her face lifted, seeing
in the curtainless window the eyebrows and skin,
herself again.

Perfect Stillness

An October morning clear
as a dish of water light swims in.
Sycamore is still a little green
and sweet gum's stars twirl
in free fall to the ground.
                                It's easy
to see how separate each thing is
and how there is no pain in it.
The hillside like a butcher's yard,
red washed away after rain,
the skeletons, for once,
still whole and standing there.
Morning has to leave us
with another grasshopper or praying mantis
rigid on the screen door,
                            a lesson again
in the perfect stillness we practice for
at night. So why does anybody cry
beside the lily pond covered with leaves
yellow and thin as a carpet
in an upstairs room?
                              Not because of dying but
because the goldfish sparks and sparks
the heavy waters of its pond and no one sees.
For yourself you want
                      what?
Friends? A hundred lovers? Or one man's eyes
steady as an angel's flame to watch you
walking on the wet grass toward a dandelion
afloat and glowing
                          just like the spot of light
caught every night between the curtains,

the one that fools you
by vanishing with your dreams.

A Kind of Goodbye

I could have sat and watched you all afternoon in the
      darkening
brought on by a summer storm bundled in the sky
like the robes of saints in frescoes.
Leaves were tossing themselves
as your fever burned out. They were pale
as your arm suspended over the edge of the bed.
All the heat of the last three days
was gone. You had the blanket up to your neck,
your eyes were closed but sleep
had taken itself away as simply as a plane
in the end takes even its shadow
from the ground. I will always remember
I didn't do what I wanted.
On the tv black-coated figures
moved through a pale street
of cobblestones, the only sound
a faint scuffle, then the harsh clang
of a horse's hard shoes on stone, far away
and beautiful in a way we'll become used to.
It made it easier to leave, to pull
the solid wood door open, to walk out
on the stone step and swing
the green door toward me.
You watched me pulling the door
to the jamb, letting go
of the knob so the lock blundered home.
We were both gone
in the same instant,
the green door so heavy and thick both sounds—
walking on gravel, creaking of a bed
as weight was given up—

might have been miles apart, maybe
not happening at all.

The Intimate Earth

The Chinese know the space inside us
where the intimate earth of the eye
is painted as delicately as silk.
A land of mist,
pines twisted from years of wind.
Rocks cling to the moss that covers them
and pilgrims go far into the mountains to dwell in caves.
All this empties itself in grief,
gives up the tiny planes of a wasp's wing,
moist soil, apricot blossoms,
and the last curl of a wave.
The broken woman rises from sleep,
looks out her window,
and has no name for anything.

No Telling

Every year before Christmas
death, it seems, throws down
more tight nets than ever before
and pulls harder, like the moon,
on everyone. There is no telling
who lays a pistol, one bullet
in a briefcase and goes to work,
which one rattles pills
in the cup of a hand for hours
and who spends seven nights
before the mirror touching
the razor's edge then lying
smoothly in the tub,
the porcelain a little like the feel
of faith, cool and unsurprising.
The beauty of it is there isn't any
question anymore, only the inevitable
rising of the wind that combs the trees
knowing what is lost
is lost and this, the thin branches
holding no secrets, is all there is.

Perfect in Its Purpose

Only two sounds: wind chimes
trembling at the ends of string like fingers
searching the skin of something new
and across the street a chain
swings inside the graveyard.
Not scary for once,

for once the night has nothing
to hide. Slick obelisks
and small arched stones stand
in a street light's diaphanous light.
The stones glow softly,
just enough to show

they have no words
for the dead who want nothing
from this world anyway
since the body is gone
and with it the chance
of picking up a crow's dropped feather
and giving it back to wind.

Such a little loss
because with tongue and teeth
you can't say anything
to make the iron dog leave
the grave it's lying on,

perfect in its purpose

like sorrow, to be there
long after the moon has washed the streets
and left them drifting
in other people's forgetful sleep.

One River

It isn't enough to pull the curtain edges together tight as a seam, as two hands over a face, and sit in the rocker with the light on. Dusk sidles like a millipede along the baseboard and is impossible to keep out or to keep from touching, for the rest of the night, the table top and picture frames with an old woman's desire for hard surfaces.

Listen how rain taps and rattles the loose glass in the window till I answer aloud with its name *rain*, open the front door and stand on the porch to watch rain make the street light slick, rain sweep with a shine as sharp as an officer's torch pinning a suspect to the roof. Silver beads gleam like a baby's toy and ricochet like shot from car hoods, asphalt, tin.

The sound of rain is the sound of drapery touching itself fold by purple fold at the wind's direction. Lightning drops and spreads dye-white through the watery black. Thunder doesn't want to cease its roar low and long in the throat like a cat that lies on the bird it batters and purrs with satisfaction.

This beauty is ambiguous as cries and thumps penetrating brick to wake me listening hard, brushing my palm over the stiff hairs on my skin. The rain rains hard and I can't tell if the cry is tires skidding on the main road,

the night finding its bruises, or the end of love. I'm alone looking into the house across the street, seeing a man glide through the room carrying nothing. He vanishes and the frame of light remains like the whole encapsulated world of an angelfish that doesn't drag even a shadow past the glass.

But all around the lighted room the dark house hulks and through the doorway night eddies in and out, one river that holds us and pulls in one direction through your life

to the other side of mine. Inside my door is a stair pleated with light, a room at the top dimly swirling around pale curtains and a raised sash, the invisible screen meeting the fading storm. I look straight through:

high up beyond us lightning's cool blue illuminates a fretwork of gray-green trees as intricate as the cricket's wings now begining to crumble sharp, unmelodious notes into the shadow floating over us. Thunder miles away mumbles into another ear. A nighthawk creaks in the deep. Without seeing them, it's certain insects spin in new-born currents of air.

Alba

The lovers rise from bed and leave
a fire banked in ashes,
stars dim and disappearing
as night unpins and drops
its faded cloth.

Each in a silence hears
a tattered fluttering across the field.
Dried leaves quivering with whispers,
what's to come, what's to come?

No light, but the road
goes forward in both directions.
No fire but burning

alive between heaven and earth.

Perceptible Breath

Frost last night.
The squash in black rags,
a few red peppers on dead plants.
You stand with your coat thrown over your robe
arranging it all into your own tableau. You choose

ironweed purpling the ditch across the road,
an empty field.
Erupted, pockmarked ground

is what you contemplate
while a bluebird draws its stitchery
from wire to leafless bramble back to wire.
And while, without your knowing it,

your breath becomes the infinite
extension from you to the sycamore's white
tangle of branches and on
to the wished-for heaven.

The Dark Ones Are Here to Help

New bedroom curtains gag the window
with gargantuan roses jeweled with dew drops
flies can drown in.
I may be smothered by morning,

if not by these then by my dreams. Long, corrupted
images explaining how I don't know how
to live my life.

Dreams, leave me alone
with the plentiful, fleshy tongues tsk-ing
over my choice. Unhappiness

twists like a rogue hair from my forehead,
multiplies like skin tags in my armpit, all
(I've been assured by medicos)
determined in my genes.

    So madness
is for me not only normal, but regular;
    it isn't wrong
to be conscious

of worms trod partway to pulp,
partly still writhing;
worms distributed every few inches
over the slick parking lot
while black heels and brown wingtips
stab, twist, slip from cars to hallway carpet.

What a mess, the tidy women say
wiping their shoes in the bathroom.
They love their children but can't be bothered
with anything smaller.

These are nice people.
We work together all day.
Only I would like them to notice,
the way a dream does,
that a spider's step makes the pine tree shiver.

And above us, all day, the sky
long since stopped believing window glass is in the way.
    Sky pours itself,
and where we're absent
curls itself on the rug and stays

as long as it can.
When I see it I say what I feel:

    Hello! Hello!
I can't keep you; I can't keep me
from being
    touched.

The Skin's Resistance

I know masses of air collide
and the turbulence created changes vapor
into drops so rain begins.
A tearing, irreversible release
shreds the clouds, becomes flickering drops
splattering a last clematis bloom.

Just because I know
is not enough. The soul of me looks out
on tendrils, layers of leaves
for shapes to imitate. The rational process,
thought and words, is used to convince another,
the partner, one of the pair.
Which is no more.

So let the individual alone
thrust out a hand for autumn rain
bare to her shoulder, bare to her breasts,
to her toes on the concrete floor;
she stands and sees and feels rain
prick the underside of her arm.
I'm willing to believe

rain comes out of nowhere but blank air
and is meant for nothing but to be
a miracle,

which is to be seen
rimming the separate petals of a bloom,
running off drop after drop
perpetual as a stroke,
like a hand on my thigh.

The hand that feels it's at the edge,
there's no place else to go
and even so
loves, persistently.

The Heartland

1.

There are no promises
that can be kept.
When a man dies young
his wife packs the table,
the lamps, the axe.
She starts out not looking back
or into the face of her son
who turns to wave to the house,
the dry creek, the long grass in bloom.
This is a child who believes
what his mother says,
that the Israelites entered the desert
without fear,
the fire of home
in their hearts.

2.

A man heaves bales of hay nine feet up
on top the other bales.
The muscles in his chest constrict
against his emptiness like a fist
he forced into his own face
when the fight with his mother
was an endless dance,
a blade sweeping under his feet.
Harvest is the season
when he sleeps without women,
without the thigh alongside his own
or the breast surfacing
between his hands,

when he is afraid to touch
for fear of letting go of everything
and holding on to her alone.

3.

A man buries his mother so early
in the spring and in the day
the frozen ground will not crumble
in his hand. The winter
wheat for miles moving
the land to another place,
another impossible return.
He remembers sleep
in the old house, winters
when timbers cracked
in the cold like the heart,
his mother always said, of a lonely man
under stars.

4.

Stepping down from the truck
in the east field
you find the flower
that grew outside your mother's room
where she used to rock,
her back, as usual, towards you.
The window she faces is open,
filling her lap
with a long breeze
and without meaning to at all
you are sitting down,
resting your head on her knees.

Finding a Dream

Because it was small,
because it lay fast in a valley,
was there beyond the car window
and gone,

I let fly my life
like a silver hook at the end of a shining line
and snagged that bright mystery
and carried it home with me
(the deeply furrowed field
burnished like an ornament amid spring-green hills,

a fringe of unleaved trees
on the north slope, the white

frame house with a tin roof
refractive as the surface of water
over a dark spot. Deep

front porch with caches of stiff leaves
and the carcass of a bird. Some bone,
some down, and a pin-feather stuck
straight up and quivering
like a lightning rod.

Listen, the dried leaves rustle and stir.
Hold up your palm;
breezy fingers speak)

Maybe Not What You Want
or What You Lost

It seems it's all going away.
Lazily the monarch drifts south
lighter than paper. Twisted skeins
of birds rush over the rivers
and plains to Texas and on
into jungles fixed in the black
lines of maps. Half the world
on half a page and nothing to touch
but the paper's silky sheen.

Maybe you can't live with this.
For you the starlings gather
in the silver maple's brittle crown,
creaking together like old doors opening
into rooms of windows, all the curtains gone,
the large unvarnished patch of floor
under a rug of dust.

Night spawns first in those rooms
where a woman folds and refolds her fingers
into a burning house and another will not leave
her hair alone because a man once said
it was almost alive,
so black and bright and deep
he wanted to swim in it. Like you
they know a blink is treacherous
and sleep worse than the weeping wind
rinsing the window pane blank again.

Hush. If everything you see is true,
you're saved. Water
slips over the green rocks
and through the gills of fish to a place
where you can't touch it again, it's true.
So say goodbye and close your eyes anyway.
Anytime you open them something
will be there with you,
maybe a red leaf barely anchored
to a bending branch
and there in the water another
leaf flickering, born of the steady flow.

Two Women Talking

Something like finches
exclaiming over a tray of millet.

Something like a pair of aspens
showing the pale green
and then the gray-green surfaces of leaves
to tell the wind's life story:

there is no end to it.

They talk about anything,
try to describe the impossible
like dogwoods flowering on a hill
and the hill behind it and on all sides
so pale blossoms tint the air
with a hint of green.

One says, like clouds
browsing the earth. The other says,
as if the branches held a winter's weight of snow
and you and I were outside time

like the wind
that hums along high, black wires,
giving its breath away.

In Which a Single Answer
Is Given to Two Questions:
How Big Is a Heart and
How Much Can It Hold?

It is the heart of love you want,
not the birth-given pump that trades opening
for closing time after time
like a miser's fist.

So you must go outside,
along the river,
past the last house and beyond
the railroad tracks turning away to loneliness

and still further on
into trees. Listen, the river
speaks softly, soothing itself;
look at the river falling into itself,

to a quiet comfort, to a pool
as clear as an infant's eye
in which the whole, old world
shines in a different light

and is held fast in the porous water:
a cradle for a twisted stick,
for the single mallard's flight pulling
like a needle through the edges of flesh

and even though he thinks he took himself away,
he is here, gentled
by the strokes of water striders
smoothing the surface, coaxing it open

to hold more. If you offer your hand
you have a partner in the sycamore's slim ghost
wavering in water, you have a bed
on the shale bottom, the necessary rock
under us from beginning to end.

Manatee

Your hand can hold
the shaft of a hoe, a pen,
a needle tethered to white thread,
an edge of satin turned under.

Slip-stitch, blind-stitch, a dress joined
more carefully than your own weak knees
and swollen elbow.
From the beginning a life is fingered
like a mandarin's daughter's feet
in their swaddle of cloth,
like a woman holding tweezers and smoothing
her brows:

I can change it, I'll fix it, I can make it better
than this.
But look

a letter lies
perfumed as a corpse
in its envelope. Dust
trims the hem of a wedding dress
while women tumble two-dollar shirts
hoping for silk.

Are we happy?
Even knowing that shit in a road feeds butterflies
yellow and black and quiet
as a dozen dancer's fans

it's hard to forgive the word *happy*
for prancing in your ear like a woman
in front of a mirror and the man
she will leave tomorrow.

Yet happiness happens
even to us:

a woman looks
and feels the salt spray spittle
on her face, the steady wind's rough shove.
A manatee rolls in the surf then sinks
away from its name, swimming out
further than words can reach, beyond herself
seeing the beast vanishing
like a wave finally coming to shore,
not there anymore,
                      but never gone

PAMELA KIRCHER holds a Bachelor's degree from Ohio University, a Master of Library Science from Kent State University, and a Master of Fine Arts from Warren Wilson College's MFA Program for Writers. Her poems have appeared widely in literary journals, including *Best American Poetry*, 1993, edited by Louise Glück. She is the recipient of three Ohio Arts Council Individual Artist Fellowships and has been a resident fellow at the MacDowell Colony. She lives in rural Ohio.

Produced at The Print Center., Inc., 225 Varick St., New York, NY 10014, a non-profit facility for literary and arts-related publications. (212) 206-8465